HAWAII'S *Animals &* WILDLIFE

Text and photographs by
H. Douglas Pratt

with additional photos by
**Tom Dove, Michael Walther, Brooks Rownd,
David Fleetham, and others**

Mutual Publishing

ISBN-13: 978-1939487-30-8
Library of Congress Control Number: 2014938658
First Printing, August 2014

Mutual Publishing, LLC
1215 Center Street, Suite 210
Honolulu, Hawai'i 96816
Ph: 808-732-1709 / Fax: 808-734-4094
email: info@mutualpublishing.com
www.mutualpublishing.com

Printed in South Korea

CONTENTS

Left: A green sea turtle sunning itself on Punalu'u Black Sand Beach in Ka'ū on the Big Island.

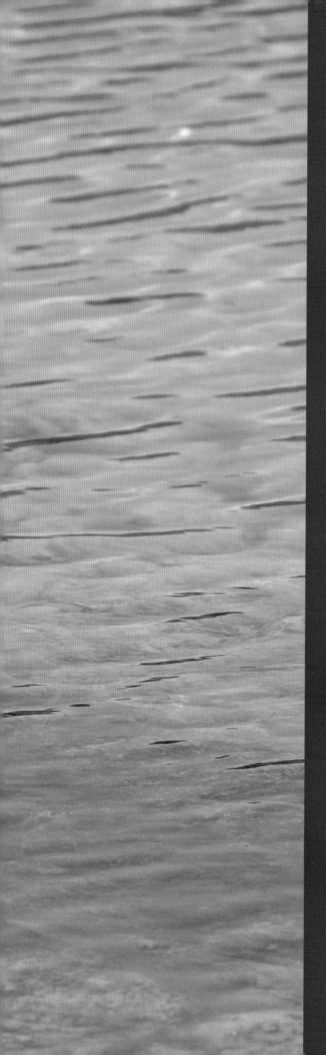

INTRODUCTION

Mark Twain called them "the loveliest fleet of islands that lie anchored in any ocean." The Hawaiian Islands remain iconic today, but they are much different from the islands Twain knew, and still more altered from those that greeted the first Polynesian settlers a millennium ago. Today's islands are home to a rich mixture of wildlife that includes native species alongside many brought in from around the world, a fauna that in this respect resembles the islands' modern human population. The first people to arrive were Polynesians who found a huge array of species that neither they, nor any other humans, had ever seen before. Many of the seabirds that nested abundantly on these predator-free islands and ranged widely over the Pacific Ocean would have been familiar, but the land animals were mostly the descendants of a few ancestors fortunate enough to survive the 2,500 mile ocean crossing. These midocean mountaintops are much younger than the surrounding continents, and were sterilized at birth by volcanic heat, so living things had to come from elsewhere, and had to be able to swim, float, or fly. No reptiles or amphibians, and only two mammals, a seal and a bat, survived the crossing, so birds became the predominant element in the islands' wildlife and remain so today. The Polynesians brought their domestic dogs, chickens, and pigs, and transported the first rats and lizards as stowaways. With the arrival of Europeans and Asians came most of our familiar domestic animals, many of which established feral (wild) populations. Later generations introduced many other species, purposely or not, for a variety of reasons, some good, some bad. The following pages showcase a representative sample of Hawai'i's most conspicuous, interesting and beautiful animals.

Left: A Nēnē, or Hawaiian Goose, wading in a Big Island estuary. Although Nēnē feed mostly in open upland habitats, if water is nearby, they take to it readily.

SEA LIFE

L ife originated in the sea, and the variety of animals that make the oceans their home may be even greater than those that live on land. The largest group of marine animals are the invertebrates—animals without backbones such as lobsters, crabs, shrimps, jellyfish, sea anemones, corals, starfish, sea urchins, clams, oysters, octopuses, squids. A book such as this cannot begin to describe these small, diverse creatures, but it can introduce some of the larger sea animals such as fish and marine mammals.

What is a fish? Surprisingly, there is no precise answer. Originally, "fish" meant any animal that spends its entire life in the water (i.e. "jellyfish," "starfish," "cuttlefish"). Today, however, "fish" usually means an aquatic animal that has gills throughout life, a backbone of some sort, and a streamlined body with fins.

We are in a golden age of fish. There are probably as many or more fish species living today than at any time in the Earth's past, and some of them, including most in this chapter, occur only in Hawai'i.

Mammals descended from fish that crawled up to live on land. Curiously, some of these land animals returned to the sea millions of years later to become our present-day marine mammals (see following chapter): dolphins, whales, and seals. Most mammals have four legs and live on land, but a few have flippers instead of legs and dwell in water. Water-adapted mammals and reptiles with four flippers, such as seals or turtles, generally retain some ties to land—they must come ashore to rest and reproduce. However, mammals with two flippers, such as whales and dolphins, are true ocean animals and cannot survive on shore.

Whitetips are not uncommon in Hawai'i and are easily identified by the white tip on the dorsal fin. Photo © David Fleetham.

Text and captions in this chapter by John P. Hoover.

Above and right: Cousins to the sharks, rays have flattened bodies, great winglike pectoral fins, and often a long whiplike tail. Unlike the bottom-dwelling stingrays, mantas swim in open water and feed on plankton. They are huge. One species attains 3,000 lbs. with a "wingspan" of over 20 ft. Most Hawaiian mantas, however, are in the 8-12 ft range. Photos © David Fleetham.

Opposite page: The odd, blade-like heads of these animals probably provide lift as the animals swim. They also bear electroreceptor organs on the underside which help the shark locate prey under the sand. Although the design may seem weird, it works: hammerhead sharks are among the most abundant and successful sharks in the sea. Photos © David Fleetham.

Above: A shark approaching a diver in Hawai'i is most likely to be this species. Bold and inquisitive, Galapagos Sharks are potentially dangerous, especially to anyone carrying speared fish. Fortunately, they are seldom encountered around the main Hawaiian Islands. Photo © David Fleetham.

Right and opposite page: Tigers are among the world's two or three most dangerous sharks. They have wide blunt snouts and dark bars on the back and sides. The bars fade on large adults, which grow to 18 ft. and weigh up to 2000 lbs. Most shark attacks in Hawai'i are the work of tiger sharks, but luckily the sharks themselves are uncommon and seldom seen. Photos © David Fleetham.

Above and right: Whitetips usually rest in caves or far back under ledges. Although they may appear lethargic, they are not harmless and should not be trifled with. Growing to about 6 ft., they typically hunt at night and are good at nabbing fish and crustaceans from their hiding places in the rocks or coral. Photos © David Fleetham.

A. Bandit Angelfish: This unusual angelfish lives only in Hawai'i.

B. Flame Wrasse: Each red and yellow male maintains a harem of red and pink females.

C. Milletseed Butterflyfish: These fish are abundant at some snorkel and dive sites.

D. Moorish Idol: With their perfect blend of form and color, they are the classic coral reef fish.

E. Spectacled Parrotfish: These large reef fish have a parrot-like beak used to scrape algae off of rock and coral and occur only in Hawai'i.

F. Wedgetail Triggerfish: Better known by the Hawaiian name humuhumu, this is the official State Fish of Hawai'i.

G. Whitesaddle Goatfish: These can be purplish, greenish, or reddish but they always have a small white spot, or saddle, above the base of the tail.

H. Yellow Tang: A school of Yellow Tangs flowing over the reef makes a gorgeous underwater sight. Photos © John P. Hoover.

13

MAMMALS

Mammals are warm-blooded animals with hair that give birth to live young, but they include marine dolphins and whales that have only a few bristles. When most mainlanders hear the word "wildlife," they think first of mammals, but the only ones to get to the Hawaiian Islands on their own were a bat and a seal. All others had help from people in one form or another. The first settlers knew only dogs, small pigs, bats, and small Polynesian rats, all of which, except for bats, they brought with them. The rats (as well as hungry people) had an immediate negative impact on nesting seabirds as well as ground-nesting land and freshwater birds. It only got worse as larger European and Asian rats came in during the 1800s. The ecology of the islands was changed forever when cattle, goats, sheep, and huge European pigs to the islands in the 1790s. These aliens ran wild in the forests and formed vast herds, converting, in a few generations, vast expanses of pristine forest to pasture. By the late 1800s, the need to preserve watersheds for sugar cane production led to control of feral animals and efforts at reforestation (although usually with non-native trees). Wild cattle are now rare, but other feral domestic animals are still common in places. In drier habitats, goats predominate, but in forests, pigs are the largest mammals today. Hawaiian feral pigs are a far cry from the little ones brought in by Polynesians, and tear up the floor of native rainforests like animated bulldozers. But pig hunting has become a cultural icon and efforts to control wild pigs always meet resistance. The mongoose, probably the most noticeable mammal in the islands, was introduced in a failed experiment to control cane field rats. Mongooses and feral cats are now the only small carnivores in Hawai'i.

One of only two native mammals (not counting dolphins and whales), the endangered Hawaiian monk seal often hauls out to sun itself on beaches and lava flows. Photo © David Leonard.

Captions for humpback whale, pilot whale, bottlenose dolphin and spinner dolphin by John P. Hoover.

Opposite page and above: Humpback whales are common around the Hawaiian Islands December to May, and can often be seen from shore spouting, splashing, and even breaching. They calve here, but do not eat. Humpbacks grow to at least 45 ft. with a weight of 40-45 tons. Only Blue, Fin, Right, Bowhead and Sperm Whales are larger. They hump their backs conspicuously just before diving, hence the name. Photos © David Fleetham.

Left and following page: A short-finned pilot whale. Despite their common name, these cetaceans are actually oversize dolphins. They are completely black except for a white patch on the chin which narrows to a line along the stomach. More apparent is the distinctive bulbous head and a dorsal fin set forward on the body. They travel in groups of 20 or more and are not uncommon in the channels between the islands and offshore. Photos © David Fleetham.

This page: Pacific bottlenose dolphins are often seen offshore. Attaining 8-11 ft., they are larger than spinners. Their distinct snout is said to have reminded sailors of the business-end of an old-fashioned gin bottle, and their face wears the perpetual smile made famous by Flipper, the TV dolphin. Photos © David Fleetham.

This page and opposite: Spinner dolphins, named for their habit of leaping out of the water and twirling in the air, are usually seen in pods of half a dozen to 250 or more. Growing to about 7 ft., they often cavort close to shore and are easy to see from land. Spinners hunt at sea at night and rest by day in shallow protected bays. Snorkelers, divers, and boaters should keep a respectful distance while they rest. Photos © David Fleetham.

Above: Monk seals are named for the fact that they lack external ears, and thus look like a monk wearing a hood.

Right: A Hawaiian monk seals look very sleek as it hauls out onto a sandy beach. Hawaiians named it 'īlio-holo-i-kauaua, which roughly translates as "surf dog."

Above: This half-grown feral pig shows the common black coat, but other colors, especially brown, are also present in the population.

Left: This handsome feral boar reveals an ancestral connection to European wild boars. Photo © Brooks Rownd.

Opposite page: The hoary bat, locally called 'ōpe'ape'a, is Hawai'i's only true land mammal. It is listed as endangered, but is not uncommon in some places. Look for them at dusk hawking insects over coastal bays. Photo © David Leonard.

Left: Arriving along with the coconut tree in which this one is feeding, the Polynesian rat is slightly smaller than the more familiar black rat and Norway rat. Photo © T. Beth Kinsey.

Below, top: Mongooses look like weasels, but belong to their own mammals family that also includes civets. Photo © Robert J. Shallenberger.

Below, bottom: The small Indian mongoose is abundant on all islands except Kaua'i and Lāna'i, but is disliked everywhere. A daytime predator, it was introduced to control nocturnal rats at which it failed miserably. But it is now the primary threat to native ground-nesting birds such as the Nēnē.

Left: Feral goats can have impressive horns.

Opposite page: A white feral goat in Kaua'i's Waimea Canyon. Grazing goats are responsible for much of the red earth we see in the canyon walls.

Above: Feral sheep are a popular game animal, but can be very destructive to native habitats. Adults vary in color from white to black, and rams have horns that spiral outward.

Left: Most feral lambs are black, some with white markings.

Above: The mouflon, a wild sheep from Europe, was brought to Hawai'i as a game animal, but local hunters prefer the flavor of feral domestic sheep! They can be seen along the Big Island's Saddle Road. Photo © John Polhemus.

Left: Horses once ran wild on the Big Island, but they did not thrive like cattle, sheep, and goats. Today they are maintained on ranches.

Opposite page: Donkeys were used as beasts of burden in Kona coffee plantations until motorized vehicles took their place. Their descendants are now feral in several spots, but efforts are being made to remove them from the wild.

Above and right: For many years, American bison have been raised for meat on a Hanalei, Kauaʻi, ranch where they can often be seen from the highway. None have escaped to become feral.

Opposite page, top: Water buffalo were used in Hawaiʻi historically as beasts of burden, and a few herds were briefly feral, but none survive today.

Opposite page, bottom: The pronghorn from North America was introduced on Lanaʻi as a potential game animal, but never did well and eventually died out.

SEABIRDS

The first inhabitants of the Hawaiian Islands were undoubtedly seabirds who came to the islands to nest even before the islands were inhabitable by land animals. It was an ideal location because they did not derive their food from the land, and no predators could take their eggs or chicks. Albatrosses, boobies, frigatebirds, shearwaters, petrels, tropicbirds, and terns nested on the islands in the millions, and may have actually led the first Hawaiian people to them. That was partly their undoing, because people and the animals they brought with them soon wiped out all but a few species of seabirds that nested on the larger islands. Today, seabirds nest mainly on predator-free offshore islets. Nevertheless, seabirds are still a conspicuous part of the island fauna, and some may even be seen far inland. Conspicuously absent are "seagulls." Gulls are temperate climate scavengers mostly in shallow coastal waters, and only a few species nest in the tropics. Mountaintop tropical islands simply do not give them what they need. A few gulls visit the islands in the northern winter, delighting local birders, but they are never common. Hawai'i's seabirds are mainly hunters that catch live prey at sea. In fact, local fishermen look for feeding flocks of boobies and shearwaters because they indicate the presence of small prey fish driven to the surface by marine predators such as the much-prized 'ahi (tuna). Among Hawai'i's top visitor attractions are several places where seabirds can be seen up close. Perhaps the best is Kīlauea Point National Wildlife Refuge on Kaua'i, but others include Ka'ena Point Natural Area Reserve and Mānana Island Overlook on O'ahu. Any headland will provide a viewpoint for boobies, terns, and shearwaters passing by, especially in the spring months.

Left: The spectacular Laysan Albatross, moli in Hawaiian, with its six-foot-plus wingspan, is Hawai'i's largest seabird. Once extirpated on the main islands, it is now nesting again on Kaua'i and O'ahu.

Above, top: This mated pair of Laysan Albatross in Ka'ena Point Natural Area Reserve on O'ahu shows the value of predator-proof fencing that protects seabird nesting sites.

Above, bottom left: Great Frigatebirds or 'iwa often fold their scissor-like tails into a point, as in this female. Males are all black.

Above, bottom right: A first-year Great Frigatebird attacks a first-year Red-footed Booby in an attempt to steal its food. Such piracy is why the bird was named for the ships once favored by pirates. Photo © Tom Dove.

Opposite page, top: The Wedge-tailed Shearwater, 'u'au kani, is the most common one in Hawai'i. It nests in burrows near the coast, and goes and comes mostly at night.

Opposite page, bottom: This grounded Newell's Shearwater was confused by lights along the shoreline and ended up on land rather than swimming on the ocean. Every fall, rescue efforts are mounted to assist such casualties of modern life.

Above, top: The Hawaiian Black Noddy differs from members of its species elsewhere in having bright orange feet, browner dorsal color, and a nearly white tail. It can be seen around its nesting sea cliffs in Hawai'i Volcanoes National Park.

Above, bottom left: The Brown Booby is the second most common booby in Hawai'i. It can be recognized by its cleancut dark brown and white color pattern.

Above, bottom right: The Brown Noddy or noio is the larger of the two noddy species in Hawai'i, characterized by uniform chocolate brown plumage, including the tail, except for a white cap.

Opposite page, top: The Red-footed Booby is the picture of grace in the air, belying its name, which comes from the Spanish "bobo" or "fool." Boobies on land are unafraid of people, hence appearing foolish.

Opposite page, bottom: The Red-footed Booby is one of the few seabirds that can still nest on the main Hawaiian Islands because it builds its nest in trees, and mongooses and dogs, at least, are not climbers.

Above: The Red-tailed Tropicbird, koa'e 'ula, nests on sea cliffs and can be seen overhead performing its somersaulting flight displays.

Right: The graceful White-tailed Tropicbird or koa'e kea feeds at sea, but it can be seen soaring over inland canyons and valleys where it nests on cliffs inaccessible to predators.

Left, top: A study in black and white, Sooty Terns nest in the thousands on offshore islets around O'ahu. Their cries of "wide-awake" can be heard when they fly over nearby shores, often at night.

Left, bottom: White, or Fairy, Terns have an odd distribution in Hawai'i. They nest only in and around the city of Honolulu, and forage mostly off leeward O'ahu.

WATERBIRDS & SHOREBIRDS

Wetlands are a scarce habitat in the Hawaiian Islands today. Because they occupy flat land near the beach, the islands' extensive natural marshes (Waikīkī was once an example), as well as most of the fishponds and taro fields built by Polynesian settlers have largely given way to condos and golf courses (whose plastic-lined ponds are too sterile to attract many waterfowl). So the habitat is now endangered, and the native birds that depend on it are, too. Fortunately, most of the remaining ponds and marshes are protected as state or federal refuges, many of which are open and accessible to the public. So while the native freshwater birds are not numerous, they are relatively easy for people to see.

Birds of wetlands can be divided for convenience into two groups, the swimmers and the waders. The first group includes familiar waterfowl such as ducks and geese, and well as duck-like birds such as coots and gallinules. The latter also frequently come out of the water and walk around on the shoreline. The Hawaiian Islands have their own unique species of ducks and geese, and each year visitors arrive from both North America and Asia. Waterfowl hunting was a popular sport in Hawai'i in the 1800s, but was outlawed when waterfowl numbers became vanishingly low. Among the native resident wading birds are one species of heron and the black-and-white Hawaiian Stilt. Again, these are joined during the northern winter by a host of visiting plovers and sandpipers that breed in the arctic. These "shorebirds" are not restricted to ponds, but may be found along shorelines of both fresh and salt water.

The handsome pink-legged Hawaiian Stilt is frequently seen, and its yipping calls often heard, in island wetlands. Photo © Tom Dove.

A

B

C

D

E

F

G

H

Above: The native Hawaiian Duck or ko-loa is related to the familiar Mallard, and on O'ahu has hybridized with it extensively. It survives in genetically pure form only on Kaua'i and a few places on the Big Island. Photo © Michael Walther.

Left: The ducklike Hawaiian Coot or 'alae ke'oke'o is the most common of the resident native freshwater birds, and can be seen on all islands. Some individuals have a red instead of white knob on the forehead.

Opposite page: A gallery of migratory ducks that visit the Hawaiian Islands each year: A Northern Pintail or koloa mapu; B Northern Shoveler or koloa moha © Tom Dove; C Ring-necked Duck; D Green-winged Teal; E Lesser Scaup; F Garganey; G American Wigeon; H Eurasian Wigeon.

Above: Nēnē swim well despite the reduced webbing between their toes.

Opposite page, top: The small Cackling Goose is the most frequent of several kinds of geese that visit Hawai'i during the northern winter.

Opposite page, bottom: The Hawaiian subspecies of Common Gallinule, locally called 'alae 'ula, often hides in wetland vegetation. It is found from Kaua'i to Moloka'i.

Above: The Wandering Tattler or 'ūlili, this individual displaying its breeding plumage, is a common sight foraging along shorelines, especially rough ones like this lava flow at Punalu'u.

Above, bottom left: The Sanderling's Hawaiian name huna kai means "sea foam" and it suits this very pale sandpiper that lives on beaches worldwide.

Above, bottom right: The Ruddy Turnstone or 'akekeke is well-named for its habit of overturning objects as it searches for prey items.

Opposite page, top: The Bristle-thighed Curlew or kioea nests in western Alaska and spends the rest of the year among the scattered islands of the tropical Pacific. In Hawai'i the best place to see it is around Kahuku on O'ahu.

Opposite page, bottom: The Black-crowned Night Heron, or auku'u, is Hawai'i's only resident heron, and here it is active throughout the day, unlike its mainland cousins. The streaked brown juveniles (left) look quite different from adults (right; © Michael Walther).

SUBURBAN BIRDS

The most familiar birds in the Hawaiian Islands are certainly those with which we share our towns and resorts. From September to April, a native species, the Pacific Golden Plover, can be found on lawns and golf courses, and may become accustomed to people and surprisingly approachable. But except for the plover, nearly all of the bird species one sees in urban and suburban settings in Hawai'i are aliens brought in from all over the world by people, and now naturalized in the islands. Many of them are colorful, or good vocalists, or both because they were popular with aviculturists, and the pet trade was a ready source. The Hawaiian Islands today host naturalized species from every continent except Antarctica, and are unquestionably the "introduced bird capital of the world". But why were so many foreign birds brought here? Through a variety of calamities, the worst of which was the introduction of mosquitoes and the diseases they transmit, Hawaiian native land birds had largely disappeared from the lowland areas where people live by the early 1900s. People like birds, and so formed organizations dedicated to bringing new songbirds to the islands to replace the lost natives. After the Nēnē and migratory ducks became scarce, hunters in Hawai'i had nothing to sustain their sport, so many game species were brought in with money from hunting licenses. As a result, the resident Hawaiian avifauna has more introduced species than surviving native ones (see Forest Birds). These non-native birds have found a home in Hawai'i, and are certainly easy on the eye and ear.

The Pacific Golden Plover nests in Alaska, but spends most of its year in Hawai'i and other Pacific islands, where it is a familiar sight on lawns, golf courses, and other open grassy places from August to May.

Above, top: The Common Myna was brought from India to Hawai'i in the 1850s as an early failed experiment in biological control. These saucy birds entertain observers in urban and rural areas throughout the islands.

Above, bottom: Large flocks of tiny blue-billed Chestnut Mannikins, a southeast Asian species, feed on grassy lawns of towns and resorts on Kaua'i and O'ahu, but are less common on other islands.

Opposite page, top: The Spotted Dove is a familiar sight in cities and towns in the Hawaiian Islands, where it was introduced from China a long time ago.

Opposite page, bottom: The little Zebra Dove, named for its stripes, can be quite tame and confiding, and its Morse-Code-like coos are one of the most familiar sounds in Hawaiian resorts and towns.

Above, top: The endearing White Tern (aka Fairy Tern or manu o Ku) is actually a seabird, but it is a common sight in and around Honolulu, where it is the city symbol. It builds no nest, and lays its eggs on bare branches of huge shade trees.

Above, bottom left: Introduced in the 1960s by cage bird fanciers, Common Waxbills in Hawai'i now form flocks so big that they resemble swarms of bees. The name refers to the resemblance of the bill to red sealing wax.

Above, bottom right: Introduced in the 1930s, the Japanese White-eye is now the most abundant bird in the Hawaiian Islands. It is usually found in small flocks.

Above, top left: The brilliant South American Saffron Finch greets visitors to the Kona Airport, and is common throughout the Kona-Kohala region. Smaller populations live on Oʻahu and Kauaʻi. Photo © Robert J. Shallenberger.

Above, top right: The North American House Finch is common in a variety of habitat from downtown Honolulu to mountain forests. In Hawaiʻi, the males vary widely from red to yellow. Females are streaky and brown.

Above, bottom: The Red-whiskered Bulbul first appeared on Oʻahu in the 1960s, but no one knows who introduced this South Asian species. It is now common throughout the island.

Following page: Red-vented Bulbuls are now one of the most abundant birds on Oʻahu, where they were introduced illegally about half a century ago.

Above, top: A big flock of Java Sparrows can overwhelm a suburban bird feeder. Otherwise, they are usually seen foraging on lawns.

Above, bottom: House Sparrows from Europe have been widely introduced around the world, including Hawai'i.

Above: The Yellow-billed Cardinal is abundant in towns and rural areas in Kona, and is slowly spreading to the rest of the Big Island. It sometimes becomes a nuisance in open-air restaurants. Photo © Tom Dove.

Left: Despite the superficial resemblance, Red-crested Cardinals are not closely related to the all-red Northern Cardinal. They live in drier, less wooded habitats including most resort areas from Kaua'i to Maui.

Opposite page: The large lime-green Rose-ringed Parakeet, native to India, is the most common of several parakeets recently introduced in Hawai'i. Hundreds come into communal roosts in downtown Honolulu, and it could become an agricultural pest on Kaua'i.

REPTILES & AMPHIBIANS

Known collectively as "herps," reptiles and amphibians are poorly represented on most oceanic islands because they are not very good at crossing large expanses of salt water. Consequently, the Hawaiian Islands hosted no terrestrial reptiles or amphibians before humans introduced them, either purposely or inadvertently. Sea turtles, however, are a conspicuous element in the islands' wildlife. They are mostly marine, but come ashore to lay their eggs and to bask in the sun. The first lizards, including four kinds of geckos and three skinks, arrived as stowaways in Polynesian voyaging canoes. Later arrivals included American anoles and even one snake, a tiny harmless wormlike animal known locally as the flowerpot snake because that was how it got to the islands in the first place. Frogs and toads did not arrive until much more recent times, but today, everything from big North American bullfrogs and South American cane toads to tiny poison-dart frogs are found in Hawai'i. New herp immigrants continue to arrive, but few of them are welcomed by islanders. Puerto Rican coqui (koh-KEE) frogs are making a nuisance of themselves with their loud nocturnal calls, and could threaten native rainforest insects and birds, and constant vigilance is necessary to prevent the arrival of dangerous snakes such as the brown treesnake, which has devastated the ecology of Guam and damaged the power grid. Nevertheless, some frogs and lizards in Hawai'i are cherished "living yard ornaments" in suburban gardens, and much loved for their control of insect pests.

Green sea turtles spend most of their lives in the sea, foraging for algae in rocky places. But they must surface to breathe as this one is doing.

Although clumsy and slow on land, green sea turtles are graceful swimmers. Photo © Cheryl King.

Left: A green sea turtle hauling out to sunbathe and raise its body temperature.

Below: The rare hawksbill sea turtle, unlike the more common green, comes to land only to lay its eggs. Snorkelers occasionally see them near coral reefs. Photo © Cheryl King.

Above, top: The strongly patterned mourning gecko often lives in close association with people. They are valued for their control of household insects.

Above, bottom: The common house gecko hitch-hiked to Hawai'i after World War II and is now very common. The sight of one running across the ceiling can be disconcerting to newcomers, but they are considered good luck in the islands.

Opposite page: The beautiful gold dust day gecko from Madagascar is a recent arrival in Hawai'i, but is spreading rapidly because people like them and transport them to new areas.

Above: The snake-eyed skink, named for its lack of movable eyelids as in snakes, has lived in rocky places near the coast in Hawai'i since ancient times.

Right: The quick-moving garden, or metallic, skink lives in a variety of habitats and is the most common skink in Hawai'i today.

Opposite page: The brown anole, a West Indian species, cannot change color like its green cousin, which it is now displacing in many places in Hawai'i.

Green anoles can be distinguished from brown anoles, even when they change color to brown, by their pink rather than orange dewlap, a flap of skin they raise in aggressive displays.

Above: The green anole, here in its brown mood, is notable for its ability to change color quickly.

Above: The little greenhouse frog is a recent import whose voice sounds like dripping water. Photo © Brent Williams.

Left: The giant South American cane toad is ubiquitous in Hawaiian gardens, and considered beneficial for its consumption of insects. Its nocturnal mating call sounds like a small motor running.

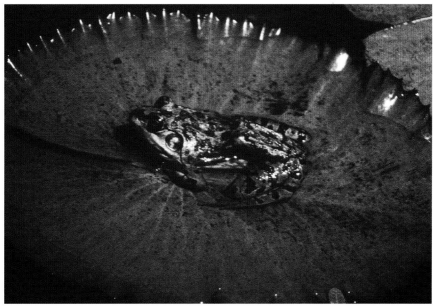

Left, top: The Puerto Rican coqui frog is spreading in Hawai'i, where its loud calls are considered an annoyance.

Left, center: The North American bullfrog is widespread in Hawaiian wetlands today, having been introduced as a food source (frog legs) over a century ago.

Left, bottom: The tiny green-and-black dart-poison frog was brought from Panama to O'ahu's Mānoa Valley in the 1930s to consume mosquitoes, but afterwards we learned that it eats mostly ants!

The Short-eared Owl or pueo is Hawai'i's only native owl. It can be mistaken for a hawk because it actively hunts by day. It eats mostly rodents. Photo © Sterling Southern.

OPEN COUNTRY BIRDS

Rural roadsides in Hawai'i are characterized by open habitats such as pastures, lawns, golf courses, and lava flows. These areas have their own distinctive bird community, made up of both native and introduced species, and these birds are among the most easily observed. During much of the year, Pacific Golden Plovers and Ruddy Turnstones, which nest in Alaska and are usually thought of as shorebirds, are a conspicuous part of Hawai'i's open country avifauna. The State Bird, the Nēnē, a species of goose found only in Hawai'i, was once nearly extinct, but captive breeding and release programs have increased their numbers dramatically and they are now often seen along roadsides on Kaua'i and the Big Island. Unlike many other geese, Nēnē are often found far from water, and the webbing between their toes is about half that of more aquatic relatives. The indigenous Short-eared Owl, found nearly worldwide, is active by day in Hawai'i and is often mistaken for a soaring hawk. The Hawaiian Hawk is found only on the Big Island, but the owl can be seen on all the islands. Chicken-like birds such as quails, francolins, partridges, turkeys, and pheasants were introduced to Hawai'i primarily as game birds. Today they often frequent resort areas and golf courses that provide them a ready source of water. Open country also supports a host of finches, sparrows, and waxbills that originated mostly from birds released by aviculturists.

Above: The Nēnē has become a frequent roadside bird on the Big Island and Kaua'i, and in Haleakalā National Park on Maui.

Right: Although they are usually seen on the ground, Nēnē can fly well.

Above: In the spring, Pacific Golden Plovers (p 33) molt into their handsome breeding plumage before migrating to Alaska to raise their chicks.

Following page, left: Juvenile Hawaiian Hawks have a distinctive pale-headed plumage. Photo © Tom Dove.

Following page, right: The Hawaiian Hawk or 'io is found only on the Big Island, where it can be seen in all but the driest habitats. This is a light phase bird, but about half of the adults are all dark. Photo © Tom Dove.

Above: The Black Francolin is the prettiest, but the most difficult to observe, of Hawaiʻi's three francolins. Look for it in drier habitats than those favored by the others. Photo © Michael Walther.

Right: The Gray Francolin, an Indian partridge, is a common sight around Hawaiian resorts where it is attracted to water sources.

Opposite page: Erckel's Francolin (FRANK-o-lin), the largest francolin in Hawaiʻi is now very rare in its native Ethiopia. It prefers wetter habitats than the other francolins.

Following page, left: The California Quail was introduced as far back as the 1850s. It is popular with hunters, and most often seen on the Big Island. Photo © Brooks Rownd.

Following page, right: Most drivers, including some Big Island residents, are surprised to see Indian Peafowl living in ranch lands along Māmalahoa Hwy. in North Kohala, but they have been established there for a long time.

Above: The Red Avadavat (ah-vah-dah-VAHT), known in the pet trade as Strawberry Finch, is an Asian waxbill that is now abundant in open country on several islands. The males seasonally lose their red coloring. Photo © Tom Dove.

Right: In dry habitats in Hawai'i, the African Silverbill can be found, often in large flocks. Its calls sound like two quarters clicked together. Photo © Tom Dove.

Opposite page, top: Many people are surprised to see the familiar Ring-necked Pheasant in Hawai'i, but it is widespread in pastures and ranch lands on several islands.

Opposite page, bottom: The Chukar is a partridge native to the Middle East. It prefers rocky places and has become "park tame" around the summit Maui's Haleakalā National Park as well as Kīlauea in Hawai'i Volcanoes National Park.

Opposite page: The Cattle Egret originated in Africa and spread to the Americas, whence it was brought to Hawai'i in the 1950s.

Above: Cattle Egrets often form large flocks that can become a hazard around airports.

Left: Wild Turkeys from North America have been in Hawai'i since the 1790s. They are often seen on ranch lands of the Big Island.

FOREST BIRDS

Except for recent lava flows, alpine zones near the summits of the highest peaks, and lowland marshes, the Hawaiian Islands were originally clothed in dense forest that varied with the amount of rainfall. These pristine forests harbored a rich bird community of species that mostly evolved in the islands (we call them endemics). Many species were lost when the first Polynesian settlers cleared lowland forests for agriculture, and habitat destruction continued with the coming of feral mammals. Ironically, the sugar cane industry, which was only possible because the lowlands had been cleared of forest, actually saved the mountain forests because of the need to preserve the watersheds. Today's lowland forests, which may look superficially like natural rainforest, are mostly artificial plant communities of non-Hawaiian trees that harbor only introduced birds. But even native forests at lower elevations harbor few, if any, native birds. Why are native forest birds found only at higher elevations? We now know that native birds thrive only where disease-carrying mosquitoes do not. Avian malaria and bird pox spread by these malevolent insects, introduced in the early 1800s, have devastated Hawaiian forest bird populations below ca. 4,000 ft. elevation. Unfortunately, as climate warms, the mosquitoes are bringing disease to higher and higher elevations and the birds' upland refuges are shrinking inexorably. Just a few decades ago, Kaua'i, which reaches barely above 4,000 ft elevation, still had all of its historically known forest birds. But several species died out since 1980, and since 2000, populations of all native birds have crashed as mosquitoes reach ever higher. Maui and the Big Island still have extensive forest above the mosquito zone, but that will change with time.

The crimson 'Apapane, one of the legendary Hawaiian honeycreepers, is the native forest bird most often noticed by people without a special interest in birds. Photo © David Leonard.

Above: The 'Apapane is one of several native honeycreepers whose wings make a noticeable cooing sound in flight. This photo reveals the squared-off outer primaries responsible for this "wing note." Photo © David Leonard.

Opposite page, top: The bright yellow 'Anianiau is found only on Kaua'i, where it is now becoming quite scarce. Photo © Tom Dove.

Opposite page, bottom: The iconic 'I'iwi, perhaps the quintessential Hawaiian honeycreeper, feeds in a native Trematolobelia on Kaua'i, where it has recently experienced a population crash. It can still be seen on Maui and the Big Island.

Above: The Kaua'i 'Amak-ihi, here plucking a grub from a native Trematolo-belia, has a bigger bill than 'amakihis on other islands. Photo © Tom Dove.

Right: The Hawai'i 'Amakihi, found on Maui and the Big Island, is probably the most common of the surviving Hawaiian honeycreepers. It is shown here in an 'ōhi'a-lehua, the dominant forest tree in the islands. Photo © Brooks Rownd.

The drab-colored 'Ōma'o sings a loud and distinctive song that is one of the dominant sounds in the Big Island's montane rainforests. It is a native thrush, the only one of five species to remain common in a few places today. Photo © Brooks Rownd.

Above: The Palila is a critically endangered finchlike honeycreeper that lives only in māmane-naio forests on the slopes of Mauna Kea. Photo © Michael Walther.

Opposite page, top: The Maui 'Alauahio is a warbler-like honeycreeper that can be seen around Hosmer Grove in Haleakalā National Park. Photo © Brooks Rownd.

Opposite page, bottom: The familiar Northern Cardinal, native to eastern North America, is widespread in Hawaiian forests but never abundant.

Above: The Hawai'i 'Elepaio is quite variable from place to place on the Big Island. This is a pale individual from the dry māmane forest of Mauna Kea. Photo © Tom Dove.

Opposite page, top: The dark form of the Hawai'i 'Elepaio is found in areas of high rainfall. Photo © Brooks Rownd.

Opposite page, bottom: The sprightly Kaua'i 'Elepaio is a native flycatcher that can still be found around Kōke'e State Park. Photo © Daphne Gemmill.

Above: The forest-dwelling Kalij Pheasant, native to the Himalayas, has become "park tame" in Kīpukapua'ulu, Hawai'i Volcanoes National Park.

Left: Feral chickens, such as this handsome rooster, are descendants of the first domestic fowl brought to Hawai'i by Polynesians. They are especially abundant in forests and on roadsides on Kaua'i, where there are no mongooses.

Opposite page: The White-rumped Shama from southeast Asia is notable for its melodic flute-like song, which can be heard on Kaua'i, O'ahu, and Moloka'i.

Above: The colorful Red-billed Leio-thrix, an Asian songbird once known as the Hill Robin, has adapted well to all types of forest in the Hawaiian Islands. Photo © Tom Dove.

Right: The Japanese White-eye is common in native forests, and some think it is competing with endangered honeycreepers.